STATE PROFILES

MONTANA

BY ALICIA Z. KLEPEIS

BLASTOFF!
DISCOVERY

BELLWETHER MEDIA • MINNEAPOLIS, MN

Blastoff! Discovery launches a new mission: reading to learn. Filled with facts and features, each book offers you an exciting new world to explore!

BLASTOFF! UNIVERSE

BLASTOFF! Beginners — GRADE K

BLASTOFF! READERS — GRADES 1-3

BLASTOFF! DISCOVERY — GRADE 4

This edition first published in 2022 by Bellwether Media, Inc.

No part of this publication may be reproduced in whole or in part without written permission of the publisher.
For information regarding permission, write to Bellwether Media, Inc., Attention: Permissions Department,
6012 Blue Circle Drive, Minnetonka, MN 55343.

Library of Congress Cataloging-in-Publication Data

Names: Klepeis, Alicia, 1971- author.
Title: Montana / by Alicia Z. Klepeis.
Description: Minneapolis, MN : Bellwether Media, Inc., 2022. | Series: Blastoff! Discovery: State profiles | Includes bibliographical references and index. | Audience: Ages 7-13 | Audience: Grades 4-6 | Summary: "Engaging images accompany information about Montana. The combination of high-interest subject matter and narrative text is intended for students in grades 3 through 8"– Provided by publisher.
Identifiers: LCCN 2021019645 (print) | LCCN 2021019646 (ebook) | ISBN 9781644873311 (library binding) | ISBN 9781648341748 (ebook)
Subjects: LCSH: Montana–Juvenile literature.
Classification: LCC F731.3 .K55 2022 (print) | LCC F731.3 (ebook) | DDC 978.6–dc23
LC record available at https://lccn.loc.gov/2021019645
LC ebook record available at https://lccn.loc.gov/2021019646

Editor: Betsy Rathburn   Designer: Andrea Schneider

Printed in the United States of America, North Mankato, MN.

TABLE OF CONTENTS

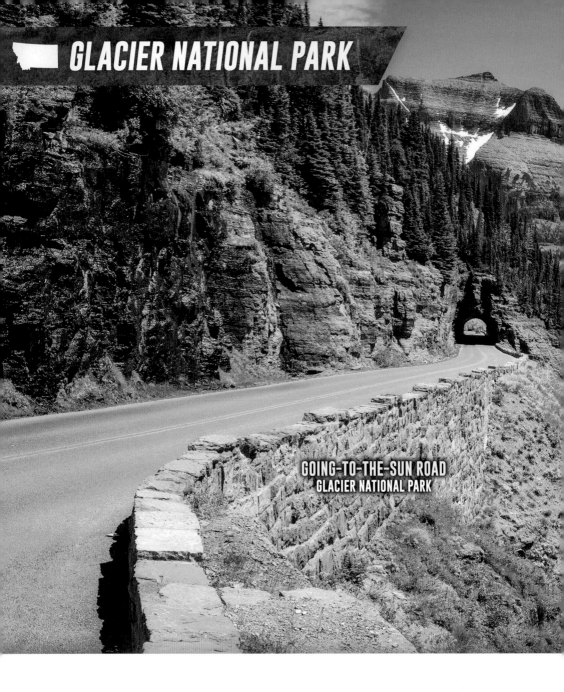

GOING-TO-THE-SUN ROAD
GLACIER NATIONAL PARK

A family arrives at **Glacier** National Park. They start with a scenic drive along Going-to-the-Sun Road. This road borders the deep blue waters of St. Mary Lake. Common loons splash about. In the distance, an elk wanders beneath the evergreen trees.

OTHER TOP SITES

FLATHEAD LAKE

GATES OF THE MOUNTAINS WILDERNESS

LITTLE BIGHORN BATTLEFIELD NATIONAL MONUMENT

MUSEUM OF THE ROCKIES

The family hikes to St. Mary Falls, where they enjoy a picnic. Later, they visit Jackson Glacier. This huge mass of ice on Mount Jackson is easy to see from the lookout point. They eat huckleberry pie and fish for dinner. Before bed, they go outside to look at the stars. Welcome to Montana!

Montana is located in the northwestern United States. It covers 147,040 square miles (380,832 square kilometers). Montana is the fourth-largest state. The state capital of Helena lies in west-central Montana, near the Missouri River. Billings, the state's largest city, sits along the Yellowstone River in south-central Montana.

Montana shares its northern border with Canada. North Dakota and South Dakota are Montana's eastern neighbors. Wyoming lies to the south. Idaho borders Montana to the south and west. This jagged border follows a line of mountains.

MISSOULA ●

IDAHO

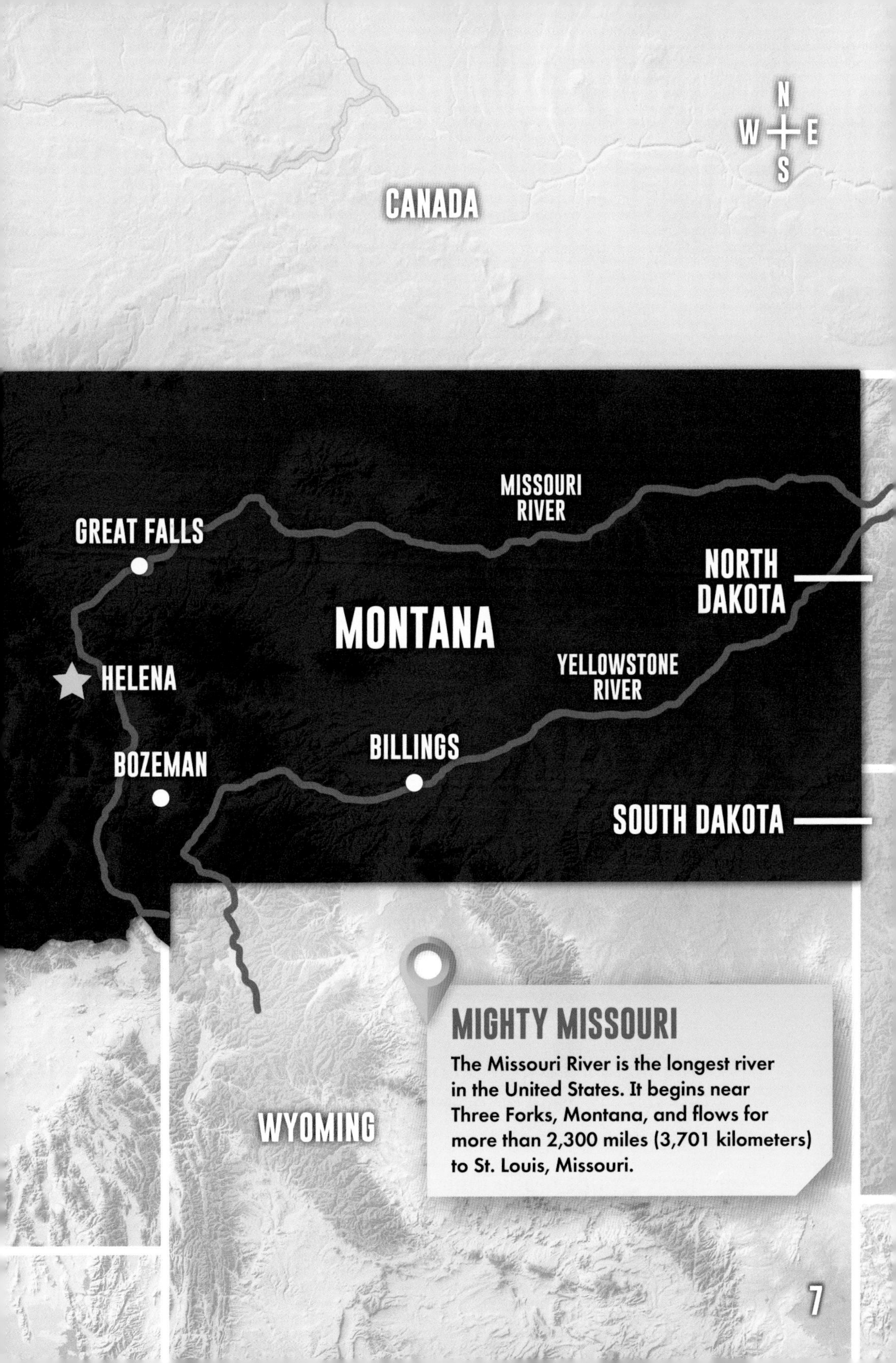

CANADA

GREAT FALLS

MISSOURI
RIVER

NORTH
DAKOTA

MONTANA

HELENA

YELLOWSTONE
RIVER

BOZEMAN

BILLINGS

SOUTH DAKOTA

WYOMING

MIGHTY MISSOURI

The Missouri River is the longest river
in the United States. It begins near
Three Forks, Montana, and flows for
more than 2,300 miles (3,701 kilometers)
to St. Louis, Missouri.

SACAGAWEA

A Shoshone woman named Sacagawea was an important member of the Lewis and Clark expedition. She helped the explorers communicate with Native Americans along their journey.

SACAGAWEA WITH
LEWIS AND CLARK

People have lived in Montana for more than 12,000 years. The first people were part of the Clovis **culture**. They made tools out of stones and bones. By the 1700s, many Native American groups made their homes in Montana. Among them were the Cheyenne, Crow, Blackfeet, Salish, and Kalispel.

The United States bought Montana from France in the **Louisiana Purchase** of 1803. Two years later, the Lewis and Clark **expedition** explored the state. Many fur traders and **missionaries** arrived in the years that followed. As more **settlers** arrived, Native Americans lost access to their hunting grounds. Montana became the 41st U.S. state in 1889.

NATIVE PEOPLES OF MONTANA

FORT PECK ASSINIBOINE & SIOUX

- Original lands throughout the Great Plains of Canada and the United States
- Around 13,000 members today
- Includes the Sioux divisions of Sisseton, Wahpeton, Yanktonais, and Teton Hunkpapa, and the Assiniboine bands of Canoe Paddler and Red Bottom

CROW

- Original lands near the Great Lakes, later moving into Montana
- Around 14,000 members today

BLACKFEET

- Original lands around the Great Lakes, later moving to northwestern Montana
- Around 17,000 members today

NORTHERN CHEYENNE

- Original lands in the Great Lakes region
- Around 11,200 members today

The Rocky Mountains cover western Montana. Narrow valleys lie between the mountain peaks. The **Great Plains** region makes up eastern Montana. The grassy landscape has river valleys, hills, and farming

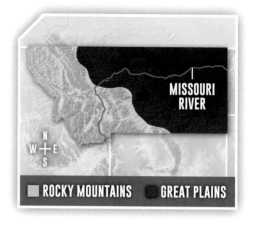

MISSOURI RIVER

■ ROCKY MOUNTAINS ■ GREAT PLAINS

fields. It also contains the unusual rock formations of the Badlands. The Missouri River cuts across northern Montana. Many of the state's other rivers drain into it.

MISSOURI RIVER

FLATHEAD LAKE

SPRING
HIGH: 56°F (13°C)
LOW: 32°F (0°C)

SUMMER
HIGH: 80°F (27°C)
LOW: 51°F (11°C)

FALL
HIGH: 56°F (13°C)
LOW: 32°F (0°C)

WINTER
HIGH: 32°F (0°C)
LOW: 14°F (-10°C)

°F = degrees Fahrenheit
°C = degrees Celsius

MONTANA'S MANY LAKES

Montana is home to many lakes. The biggest natural lake is Flathead Lake. It has 185 miles (298 kilometers) of shoreline!

Montana's climate is dry and mild. Western Montana has cooler summers and warmer winters. It is also wetter than the east, with heavy snowfall in the mountains. Eastern Montana has hot summers and cold winters.

11

BIGHORN SHEEP

Montana is home to a huge variety of wildlife. In the mountains, grizzly bears eat berries and tear apart logs in search of insects. Bighorn sheep leap among the peaks as golden eagles soar overhead. Mountain lions lie in wait to pounce on grouse or chase down moose.

GOLDEN EAGLE

Western milk snakes slither in the grasslands of the Great Plains. Badgers often hunt in the **prairie** grasses for ground-nesting birds such as bank swallows. Northern leopard frogs hop across the prairie in search of insects. Western meadowlarks fly across Montana. Trout, bass, and catfish swim in the state's many lakes and rivers.

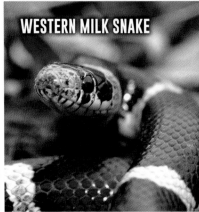

WESTERN MILK SNAKE

NORTHERN LEOPARD FROG

MONTANA'S CHALLENGE: CLIMATE CHANGE

Many Montana animals are affected by climate change. Heat waves can lead to wildfires that destroy animal homes. Less snowfall in the mountains makes it hard for animals to find water.

WILDFLOWERS

Montana has many wildflowers. Prairie smoke has bell-shaped flowers that look like smoke plumes. Beardtongue has what looks like a fuzzy yellow tongue sticking out of its violet petals.

GRIZZLY BEAR

Life Span: up to 30 years
Status: least concern

grizzly bear range =

LEAST CONCERN	NEAR THREATENED	VULNERABLE	ENDANGERED	CRITICALLY ENDANGERED	EXTINCT IN THE WILD	EXTINCT

Montana is not crowded. Only around 1 million people live there. Its **population density** is among the lowest in the nation. There are more cows than people! Most Montanans live in **rural** areas. Some Native Americans live on **reservations**. But the state's largest cities, such as Billings and Missoula, are growing.

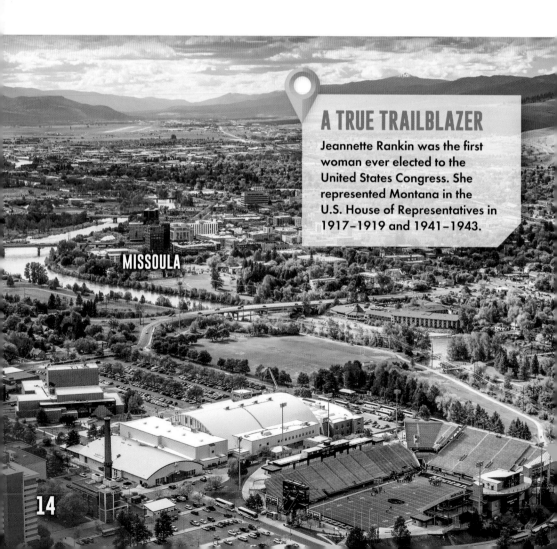

MISSOULA

A TRUE TRAILBLAZER

Jeannette Rankin was the first woman ever elected to the United States Congress. She represented Montana in the U.S. House of Representatives in 1917–1919 and 1941–1943.

FAMOUS MONTANAN

Name: Brad Bird

Born: September 24, 1957

Hometown: Kalispell, Montana

Famous For: Academy Award-winning movie director known for writing and producing *The Incredibles*, *Ratatouille*, and several other popular movies

Around 8 out of 10 Montanans have **ancestors** from Europe. Montana's second-largest group is Native Americans. Smaller groups of Montanans are Hispanic, Asian, or African American or Black. Many **immigrants** are moving to Montana. Newcomers arrive from Canada, Mexico, Germany, and China.

Billings was founded as a railroad town in 1882. The railroad brought many settlers. The population boomed. In the 1900s, the city's cattle industry grew. Billings's location on the Yellowstone River helped cattle ranches and farms grow.

YELLOWSTONE RIVER

Today, Billings is a center for business and recreation. Food processing and oil are big industries. For fun, people visit the Western **Heritage** Center to learn about Montana's history and culture. ZooMontana visitors can see animals from around the world. At the Rimrocks, people can hike high above the city!

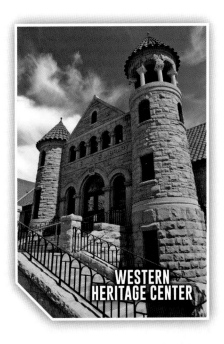
WESTERN HERITAGE CENTER

RIMROCKS

NIFTY NICKNAME

One of Billings's nicknames is Montana's Trailhead. The city has many beautiful spots to bike and hike. It is also close to several national parks.

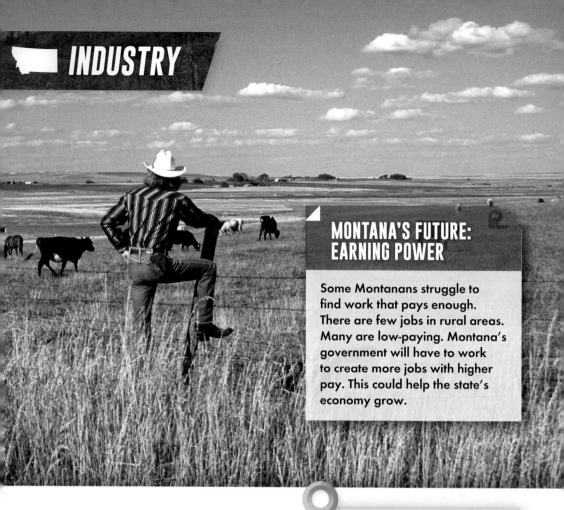

MONTANA'S FUTURE: EARNING POWER

Some Montanans struggle to find work that pays enough. There are few jobs in rural areas. Many are low-paying. Montana's government will have to work to create more jobs with higher pay. This could help the state's economy grow.

Montana's early industry was based on **natural resources**. In the 1800s, gold was discovered in the state. Coal, silver, and copper mining were also important. Ranchers raised cattle and sheep. Many Montana forests were cut down for timber.

MANY VISITORS

In 2019, over 12 million people visited Montana from other states and countries. Popular attractions include Glacier and Yellowstone National Parks and the Lewis and Clark Trail.

Today, coal and copper mining are still important. Miners also dig up talc and gold from the Rocky Mountains. Montana ranchers still raise cattle and sheep. Farmers grow wheat, hay, and barley. Northwestern Montana is the center of the state's lumber and wood products industry. Most Montanans work **service jobs**. They may work in parks, hospitals, or schools.

INVENTED IN MONTANA

YOGO SAPPHIRES
Date Discovered: 1895
Discovered By:
Jake Hoover

BOTTLE OPENER AND CLOSER
Date Invented:
patent approved in 1911
Inventor: John D. Thompson

HOLTER HEART MONITOR
Date Invented: patent approved in 1965
Inventors: Norman "Jeff" Holter and Bruce Del Mar

FOOD

PASTY

Montana is well known for its variety of meat dishes. Pasties, dough pouches filled with meat and vegetables, became popular in the 1800s. They were easy to bring into mines. Other popular dishes include elk burgers and bison meatballs. Rainbow trout may be smoked or pan-fried.

FANTASTIC FRY BREAD

Many Native American tribes, including the Blackfeet and the Crow, make fry bread. It can be eaten plain or with honey, butter, or jam.

Huckleberries are a key ingredient in many Montanan desserts. These berries are often used to make huckleberry pie. They are also used in ice cream, cakes, and even taffy. The Flathead Lake area is known for its variety of cherries. Cherry cobbler and cherry pie are popular treats!

ELK BURGER

HUCKLEBERRY PIE

CHERRY COBBLER

8 SERVINGS

Cherry cobbler is served in homes and restaurants all over Montana. Have an adult help you make this recipe.

INGREDIENTS

2 cups sweet cherries, pits removed

2/3 cup plus 6 tablespoons sugar, divided

1 cup flour

1 teaspoon baking powder

2 tablespoons cold butter

1/2 cup milk

DIRECTIONS

1. Preheat the oven to 375 degrees Fahrenheit (191 degrees Celsius).

2. In a small saucepan, bring cherries and 2/3 cup sugar to a boil over medium heat. Remove from heat and set aside.

3. In a medium-sized bowl, mix together the flour, baking powder, and remaining sugar. Add the butter and combine until the mixture looks like coarse crumbs.

4. Stir the milk into the flour mixture until moistened.

5. Spread the flour mixture into a greased 8-by-8-inch cake pan. Pour the cherry mixture on top.

6. Bake for about 30 minutes until the edges are golden and the cherry filling looks bubbly. Enjoy!

RODEO
ENNIS

Many Montanans enjoy college sports. The Grizzlies and the Bobcats football teams are popular. Rodeo events also draw crowds. Montanans also enjoy art. Art lovers explore museums and galleries in Montana's cities. The Missoula Children's Theater draws many visitors to its fun performances. The Billings Symphony Orchestra highlights music from around the world.

Montana has many outdoor activities. In the winter, the mountains draw skiers and snowboarders. Snowshoeing and ice skating are also popular winter pastimes. In warmer weather, people go hiking or fishing in state and national parks. Montana's mountains and **canyons** also attract rock climbers!

DIGGING FOR DINOSAURS

The Montana Dinosaur Trail has 14 locations that stretch across the state. Some locations show off dinosaur fossils from Montana. Others offer the chance to help dig for new discoveries!

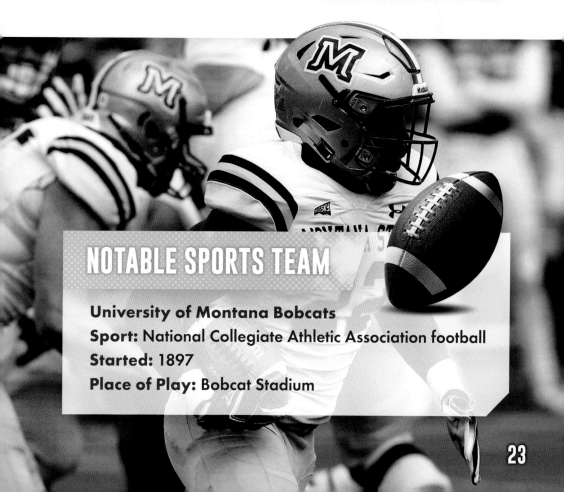

NOTABLE SPORTS TEAM

University of Montana Bobcats
Sport: National Collegiate Athletic Association football
Started: 1897
Place of Play: Bobcat Stadium

PENGUIN PLUNGE
WHITEFISH WINTER
CARNIVAL

Every February, the village of Whitefish holds its Whitefish Winter Carnival. Events include a parade and the Penguin Plunge, where people dip into Whitefish Lake's icy waters. In June, Great Falls hosts the Lewis and Clark Festival. People reenact the journey of these famous explorers. Native American drummers and dancers also perform.

Dancers, musicians, and craftspeople showcase their talents at the Montana Folk Festival in Butte each summer. At the Crow Fair in August, Native Americans show off their cattle roping and bull riding skills. Other events include a parade and dancing. Montanans celebrate their **traditions** throughout the year!

LEWIS AND CLARK FESTIVAL

CROW FAIR

SO MANY TIPIS

The Crow Fair is also called the "Tipi Capital of the World." Visitors set up over 1,000 tipis to stay in during the fair.

1910

Glacier National Park is established

1805

The Lewis and Clark Expedition crosses the area that will become Montana

1876

Native American tribes defeat U.S. troops at the Battle of Little Bighorn

1862

John White and his partner discover gold at Grasshopper Creek, leading to a mining boom

1916

Montanan Jeannette Rankin becomes the first woman elected to the U.S. Congress

1889

Montana becomes the 41st state

1964

Heavy rains rupture dams, causing flooding through much of Montana

2011

The Silvertip Pipeline bursts, spilling thousands of gallons of oil into the Yellowstone River

2020

The Bridger Foothills wildfire burns more than 8,200 acres of land and destroys 28 homes

2001

Judy Martz becomes the first woman to serve as Montana's governor

MONTANA FACTS

Nicknames: The Treasure State, Big Sky Country

Motto: *Oro y Plata* (Gold and Silver)

Date of Statehood: November 8, 1889
(the 41st state)

Capital City: Helena ★

Other Major Cities: Billings, Missoula, Great Falls

Area: 147,040 square miles (380,832 square kilometers);
Montana is the 4th largest state.

Population

1,084,225
(2020)

STATE FLAG

Montana's flag is dark blue. Across the top is the word Montana in gold letters. In the center of the flag is the state seal. It features a bright sun, mountains, a forest, and the Great Falls of the Missouri River. A shovel and pick represent the mining industry, and a plow represents farming. The state motto is written at the bottom of the seal.

INDUSTRY

Main Exports

 wheat

 beef

 chemicals

 grain products

 beverages

JOBS

MANUFACTURING
4%

FARMING AND NATURAL RESOURCES
8%

GOVERNMENT
14%

SERVICES
74%

Natural Resources
fertile soil, timber, coal, oil, natural gas

GOVERNMENT

Federal Government

2 REPRESENTATIVES | **2** SENATORS

MT

USA

4 ELECTORAL VOTES

State Government

100 REPRESENTATIVES | **50** SENATORS

STATE SYMBOLS

STATE BIRD
WESTERN MEADOWLARK

STATE ANIMAL
GRIZZLY BEAR

STATE FLOWER
BITTERROOT

STATE TREE
PONDEROSA PINE

ancestors—relatives who lived long ago

canyons—deep and narrow valleys that have steep sides

culture—the beliefs, arts, and ways of life in a place or society

expedition—a journey with a purpose, such as to explore an area

glacier—a massive sheet of ice that covers a large area of land

Great Plains—a region of flat or gently rolling land in the central United States

heritage—the traditions, achievements, and beliefs that are part of the history of a group of people

immigrants—people who move to a new country

Louisiana Purchase—a deal made between France and the United States; it gave the United States 828,000 square miles (2,144,510 square kilometers) of land west of the Mississippi River.

missionaries—people sent to a place to spread a religious faith

natural resources—materials in the earth that are taken out and used to make products or fuel

population density—a measure of how crowded a place is based on the number of people per square mile

prairie—large, open areas of grassland

reservations—areas of land that are controlled by Native American tribes

rural—related to the countryside

service jobs—jobs that perform tasks for people or businesses

settlers—people who move to live in a new, undeveloped region

traditions—customs, ideas, or beliefs handed down from one generation to the next

TO LEARN MORE

AT THE LIBRARY

Gregory, Josh. *Montana*. New York, N.Y.: Children's Press, 2019.

Mattern, Joanne. *Glacier National Park*. New York, N.Y.: Children's Press, 2018.

Wilson, Wayne L. *The Blackfeet*. Kennett Square, Pa.: Purple Toad Publishing, 2017.

ON THE WEB

FACTSURFER

Factsurfer.com gives you a safe, fun way to find more information.

1. Go to www.factsurfer.com.

2. Enter "Montana" into the search box and click Q.

3. Select your book cover to see a list of related content.

INDEX